Just Enough

Growth House, Inc.
www.growthhouse.org

JUST

ENOUGH

Collected Writings of an Old Gangster

Nancy Jaicks Alexander

To My Fellow/Fella
Villagers
        Blessings!
    Nancy Jaicks Alexander
        ~aja 09

Published by Growth House, Inc.
www.growthhouse.org

Designed and edited by Les Morgan
Front cover photograph by Nancy Jaicks Alexander
Back cover portrait by Colette Urquhart

Cataloging Data:
Jaicks Alexander, Nancy
Just Enough: Collected Writings of an Old Gangster / Nancy Jaicks Alexander
BISAC: Biography & Autobiography / Personal Memoirs

15.24 x 22.86 cm.
ISBN-10: 1453891684
ISBN-13 978-1453891681
First Edition: Berkeley, 2010

 Paper made from 30% post-consumer waste recycled material.

To His Holiness the Fourteenth Dalai Lama

To my children, Donald and Mary

To Les Morgan

Contents

PREFACE

I love to parse words. PRE — FACE.

Original face — what was your face before you were born? A profound Zen Buddhist question. The first time I learned of it decades ago I was stunned. I had never considered such an ego shattering idea. So here I am writing straight out from my ego in the hopes that what follows will please you. These writings — musings, meditations, and tales, with some memories thrown in — are for friends and family. I do not seek a wider readership, but I do seek to be seen by you and by myself too.

Words on a page give me a face — a now-face — always with the pre-face looking over my shoulder.

INTRODUCTION

It's taken seventy-seven years to be me. Not an easy time, a good part of it.

I was "to the manor born" in 1933 in Lake Forest, Illinois. That world of material wealth, private schooling and debutante balls was lost due to the mismanagement of family inheritances by my alcoholic father. There was an auction held in my home and all of its contents were sold. We had to give away my beloved black Persian cat because we were moving from a seven-bedroom house into a two-bedroom apartment, with no pets allowed.

From the age of eight I dreamed of becoming a professional actress. In 1952, I attended Northwestern University's Theatre School. I won the freshman best-actress award playing Stella in an extended scene from "A Streetcar Named Desire". Early the next year, I became immobilized with depression and dropped out of school.

I escaped from that quagmire by moving to San Francisco in 1953. My first job was as a shop girl selling cosmetics at the Elizabeth Arden Salon. Miss Arden liked to hire the likes of me — down-and-out debutantes. I redeemed myself in the eyes of my mother and Lake Forest society by marrying a Harvard lawyer in 1956. We had a beautiful son and daughter.

In the fifteen years that the marriage lasted I had twelve years of Freudian analysis. The analysis gave me the beginnings of a sense of self but eventually both the marriage and the therapy became stifling. I left both in the same month.

I moved to Berkeley from San Francisco with my children in 1971. Part of my motivation for the move was that the Berkeley School System had been integrated for six years, but San Francisco was just beginning the process. As a single parent I wanted my children to have a stable school environment. The Elmwood neighborhood that we moved into reminded me of Chicago's beautiful Northshore with gracious elm trees and century-old shingled-houses.

For the next fifteen years, I had various odd jobs. Two stand out. One was as a soda jerk at Ozzie's Elmwood Soda Fountain. The other was an unpaid job serving on the KQED Board of Directors (1976-1980). Both jobs were important to me, in very different ways. At Ozzie's I took the orders, served the food, and washed the dishes. I had nothing hanging over me when I went home at night. The KQED Board was very different. Because I had never been in an elected public position I constantly questioned my competence. I regard the Public Broadcasting System (PBS) as one of the most important instruments of freedom of speech in our democracy. There are persistently those who would curtail it or shut it down. Please, dear reader, always help to support and protect that system.

Esalen Institute at Big Sur, California, is the the midwife of the human potential movement. In 1981 I spent a year in residence at Esalen as a Work Scholar. I studied Gestalt Therapy, Encounter Group Dynamics, Psychodrama, and honed my intuitive gifts. At the end of my year of residency, the Institute's psychic told me, "Your life's work is Elisabeth Kübler-Ross." I knew who she was, of course, and respected her work, but had never met her. In surprise, I asked, "Should I write her a letter and tell her that a psychic had told me to work with her?" The psychic replied, "Send the letter! If it's supposed to happen, the universe will take care of it." I wrote the letter. To my astonishment, I got a letter back within a week from Elisabeth's secretary. He suggested that I come and participate in one of her five-day "Life, Death and Transition" workshops, which I did in Spring of 1982. In the Fall of that year Elisabeth asked me to begin training to become a member of her staff. I became a full member of her international teaching and workshop staff in 1985. I was one of only three people on a staff of fifty who were not licensed therapists or medical practitioners. I left Elisabeth's staff in 1993, shortly after the death of Robert Evans Alexander, my second husband. Elisabeth discontinued the workshops in 1994. She died in 2004.

Bob was the love of my life. I met him at Big Sur and we married in 1984. I was a child bride — I was fifty-one and he was seventy-six. (Dr. Freud, I finally got to marry my father.) My father and Bob had so much in common. Bob was as handsome as my father, with the same flashing blue eyes. They were both builders, my father of roads and bridges, and Bob as an architect. Both of them were Sagittarians. They were dreamers and creators.

In 1991 Bob and I were among the co-founders of the first prison hospice in the world, at Vacaville Medical State Penitentiary for Men. The hospice project was an outgrowth of a support group that I facilitated there for seven years for inmates with AIDS. My background as a member of Kübler-Ross' staff gave credibility to the proposal by the Catholic Chaplain, Father Patrick Leslie, to open a hospice inside the prison. Bob was always present and supportive of me and the men. He was a strong father-figure for the inmates with AIDS and the hospice volunteers. The men identified with him as a rebel. Bob died in November of 1992. The California Department of Corrections and Rehabilitation dedicated the hospice to him in 1993. From 1991 to 2010 I continued to serve there. I went to the prison once a week to meet with and train the inmate hospice volunteers. I retired after twenty-five years (and two days) on November 5th, 2010. In all of my writings about the prison I have changed names and details to protect the privacy of inmates.

My professional life as a consultant on issues of trauma, grief, and hospice is now over. Aging is a profound time of "letting go" and being deeply open to what is next. I am creakier but content.

Acknowledgements do not go far enough. I am so graced by my teachers who encourged me along this writing path. They are Pat Schneider of Amherst Writers and Artists, Joan Marie Wood of Temescal Writers, Tom Spanbauer of Dangerous Writing, and especially Autumn Stephens of Yellow Tablecloth. Their great skill and heart call out for very deep thank-yous from me.

My daughter, Mary Friend Doane, patiently and lovingly listened to all my lamentings and reviewed the final draft. My dear friend, Les Morgan, prodded me at every turn with gentle tenacity and magically put it all into the form that you now hold. To both of them, thank you for your loving support. My gratefulness knows no bounds.

Nancy Jaicks Alexander

November, 2010

Berkeley, California

PRAYERS THAT GUIDE MY LIFE

BODHISATTVA PRAYER

As long as space remains,
As long as sentient beings remain,
Until then, may I too remain
To help dispel the miseries of the World.

Shantideva

BE PATIENT

Be patient toward all that is unsolved in your heart
And try to love the questions themselves.

Do not seek the answers that cannot be given you
Because you would not be able to live them
And the point is to live everything!

Live the questions now.

Perhaps you will gradually, without noticing it,
Live along some distant day into the answers.

Rainer Maria Rilke

Some People Die Young

Some people,
sweet and attractive
and strong,
happen to die young.

They are masters in disguise
teaching us about
Impermanence.

His Holiness The Fourteenth Dalai Lama

THE MIRROR OF MY HEART

I cleansed the mirror of my heart.

Now it reflects the moon.

Zen Master Renseki

Written in 1789, the year of his death

AUTOBIOGRAPHICAL

HOW MANY HUMPS ON THE CAMEL PACKAGE?

I grew up surrounded by cigarette smoke. Both my parents were Camel smokers. Every Saturday at the movie matinees, I watched icons like Humphrey Bogart with his foggy, pushy voice, Veronica Lake looking languidly through her long blonde bangs, and Sinatra singing of "lipstick traces". The ads in magazines and on the radio all pushed a mythology of sexual power. Smoking was for grownups. Smoking was sexy. I smoked my first cigarette at six at Emilie's house. We sat in the study and coughed until we hurt and neither of us touched one again until we were sixteen. It took me thirty years to finally quit.

But I digress. I really want to tell you about the cigarette boxes. There were two of them, solid silver that held three packs neatly side by side. The boxes were a wedding gift to my parents. Each was engraved on the bottom with my parents' names, the date of their betrothal and the name of the gift giver which I came to see as a true symbol of my Uncle Stanley who owned everyone and everything. As a child I loved those boxes. One sat in the living room, the other in the study, each always carefully filled. Their design was heavy with embossed fat cherubs in a forest dancing over every inch of all the visible sides. I loved to pick up and hold their smooth elegance and wonder at the dancing figures. I loved the smell of the fresh tobacco as each package was carefully opened before it went into the box. Most of all, I loved the discreet sound the box made when I closed it.

I inherited those boxes and gave one to each of my children when they married — a gift of lives and loves and memories long gone.

One January my daughter's home was broken into and her box was stolen. It still breaks my heart.

MRS. NOBLE

Mrs. Noble was sparse of frame and flesh, but determined of will and hard work. She was our laundress. By the time I had memory of her I was eight or nine, living in an elegant old Victorian with an open veranda on two sides, a three story tower on one front corner and a separate garage which had been the original barn at the back of the house. Even with its seven bedrooms and three stories it was modest in size compared to some other houses in my Chicago suburban home town.

She came on Thursdays descending to the basement that was cold and dark. There was a furnace room, a coal bin, a laundry and drying room and dark storage spaces that I quickly avoided whenever down there with her.

In her domain, besides two wash tubs was a one-agitator washing machine and a mangle. I can still recall the thub-thub-thub of the washer, but what brings my memory fully alive is the mangle. She pressed all of the household linens on it, shirts, blouses, underwear and lingerie and many other unknowns to me now. I remember the heat from the mangle. As she pressed large sheets the steam rising from the damp cloth would encompass my face, eyes and nostrils. "Stand safe," she would say. I loved to watch her agile hands guiding the cloth to perfect smoothness and folding.

But what I loved best was teatime with her. At mid-afternoon she came up to the kitchen's sun porch and made herself tea.

Mrs. Noble was Scottish-born and I learned from her the ritual of teatime. No teabags, of course, but hot water poured from a cozied pot over leaves held in a silver strainer into a fragile china cup. The liquid gold tea shone brightly in the clear white bowl. Half a dozen or so enticingly-

18

escaped leaves lay at the bottom of my cup. At first not seen because of cream and sugar, but revealed when my tea was drunk.

I sat solemnly and politely opposite her on the bright porch waiting eagerly for her to say, "Let's see yer cup now." Her soft Highland burr always entranced me. There in my cup lay a mystery to be revealed. I'm sure she never told of any clear events to come or great insights, but what she did do was to open the door to the Great Mysteries for me and unbeknownst back then, set me on a path that I travel to this day — loving The Mysteries and endlessly watching for their Secrets to be revealed.

ED

September, 1968.

This piece is about leaving my first husband.

The little boy is shy. His face reaches out to you from the picture, tender, soft and gentle. His head is slightly cocked and it almost looks phony, as though he had learned to be sweet to fight the world. His hand holds the pummel, showing the form of the man to come. Only his right leg is visible, hanging down languidly, making no attempt to fit the stirrup. His knee is dirty, his shoe is scuffed, and his knee sock slightly wrinkled.

I love this little boy, city-bred, who somehow looks quite accustomed to the rented pony. His shy being is focused on the camera and probably his mother standing beside the hooded photographer. His lips are soft and faintly smiling. His eyes are veiled by heavy brows that shut out the world or prevent the world from looking in.

"Mama, Mama," he pleaded, "read to me, please read to me." I heard that little boy beg to his mother and for the first time through fifteen years of love and hate of this man the wall was broken through.

We had been separated for four months and he had come at my request to my therapist. It was brave of him and through the long session, she had gradually broken down his veiled wall and there, as he lay cradled in her lap on the floor, he asked for what he had never gotten, his Mama.

I had tried every way I knew how to pierce that veil and breach that wall. In the end, to survive, I fled. I fled in desperation for he only wanted the frightened little girl to remain. He, unwittingly, was killing the woman who wanted to live. He grasped and squeezed the life from her. I

20

fled, leaving hurt and pain in my wake, but I was running for my life, for air, for sunshine.

Where did the tender little boy go? He is there, but buried in bitterness, hate and revenge.

Sitting on the witness stand, the eyes of the judge, my attorney, and the bitter little boy are on me. Ed said, "*You?* Upset by the divorce? You are the one who wanted it!" The pain behind his words echoed to me, "Mama, Mama! Read to me! Please read to me!" I wanted to scream, "No, no, I didn't want it." I wanted the bitter little boy to crumble. I wanted life flowing from his limbs, I wanted laughter, I wanted bodies hot and sweaty, playing and loving, I wanted fights to relieve tensions and weeping to share joy. It never came, it never happened. The dream died before it was born. I mourn — I mourn daily the folly that tried to be real. It never was, it never could be.

Ed — reach out, reach out for the life that you were denied. The past is very dead, but you must go back, back to the infant who screamed because he was wet or hungry. Scream, kick, and yell because you didn't get what you needed. Free your voice, free your body. You are bound up by frustration, rage and fear. It is safe. There are those who have the tools to show you the way. You cannot know peace and flowing until you relieve and release the rage.

I love you Ed. I love the little boy who was denied so much. I love the man you sometimes are, but you must find your own way.

You must read to yourself.

NINI

How come I got these twenty-six years more and she didn't?

Paul called late one afternoon in the Fall — she'd had a stroke, was in the ICU at San Francisco General and he wanted me to come.

A stroke — my god she's only forty-seven — how can that be! I drove into The City shaken with trepidation — Nini, my Nini — my buddy since we were six.

She was tall and graceful — dark tumbling curls, long elegant legs and a voice of velvet. She called me "Nanikins" sometimes, which I loved. She came from money and her taste in wines, cars, clothes and men (well not so much men) reflected it.

Her name was Frances (after her mother), Eugenie (after Napoleon's Empress), Faitoute (after her father) Gooding (ever commemorated by the proud Revolutionary song).

She always pushed Calder's mobiles into action, which brought museum guards running She would then grandly announce Calder had instructed her to do so if she ever came across one that wasn't moving. She gave Valentine's Day Party Scavenger Hunts that had us running all over San Francisco looking for erotic foods, libations, and literature. We also celebrated Bastille Day with her by drinking Calvados and eating cheese that reeked of a French barn yard. She was fluent in French and smoked dope with e. e. cummings.

She and I hitchhiked through southern Ireland in 1973 — she 6'1", I 5'9" — tall enough over anyone we thought might be a problem. We had

22

rented a horse and caravan, but gave both up after four hours — the horse, "Shayla", being smarter than both of us — used our thumbs the rest of the way. We went to a steeplechase in a farmer's fields and she tried to bet, but they wouldn't let her, told her all the races were fixed — we went to a poetry reading in Kinsale and met Marigold Slowcock who served us Tulomore Dew the next morning, sitting in her kitchen with her dog Barbara.

We sat on my back patio up on Twin Peaks and drank Gallo Red, ate Molinari Salami with hunks of swiss cheese and talked about masturbation. My psychoanalyst was shocked when I told him, he said women don't talk about those things with each other. (This was 1958 or so). He didn't know Nini or me for that matter!

She lived on and off in Paris for years — worked for that city's VIP visitors' bureau and toured many dignitaries around, the only non French-born guide! But she finally settled on Potrero Hill in San Francisco, reveling in its then blue-collar aura.

There would have been more, endlessly more, but damnit, like her life, it was cut short. It was an aneurism in her brain. I was the executor of her estate and among her papers I found a horoscope done for her at her birth. The time allotted to her stopped in her fifth decade.

Today is her birthday, March 7, 2007.

BIOGRAPHY

A short biographical note, written October 11, 2006.

It was, so I was told, a wet and cold night, late March, close by the shores of Lake Michigan in northern Illinois. I was not supposed to arrive until the end of May — I've been arriving early to every event ever since.

I want to tell you about late in my life now. I'm 73, a widow, mother, grandmother, lover of floating hawks, Big Sur, the Dalai Lama, Chappaquiddick Island and an impossibly cute eight-week old miniature poodle who lives next door, named Pepper.

I have counseled the dying and those who love and/or attend them for many years.

I love the gift of sharing with others the beauty that lies within each of us.

I am very frightened for our Planet now. What we are leaving our grandchildren at times overwhelms me.

I look to calm meditation — to the Buddha sitting under the Bodhi tree and chocolate for comfort.

CRUCIBLE

These are two separate pieces that are connected.
The July piece is a reflection on the earlier May writing,
which was written when I was in a depressed mood.

May 3, 2003

Yesterday, with the Talking Stick in my hand I walked again into the Crucible of those first six weeks of my life. The agony of the loneliness there shaped my life's path. All the succor and strength that I have sought down the years is there too, of course, and so as I write this morning I breathe in prayerful air that blesses me with enveloping compassion.

On my puja table sits a three hundred year old Tibetan singing bowl. Out of its emptiness comes its usefulness. Out of my emptiness comes my usefulness.

అోఁ

July 1, 2003

I am stunned. Since that May day I have been enveloped by my wandering heart's lostness.

Loneliness. I cannot shake the void. I am just sitting. At first, seeking change, expansion, openness, and praying. But now, just waiting. Being — nowhere to go — there. Empty. Waiting.

Crucible, burning bright.

THE SWING

October 18, 2006.

Huntington Park on Nob Hill is elegant with a confident sense of self. It is surrounded by San Francisco icons — Grace Cathedral, The Pacific Union Club, the Masonic Center, and cable cars rattling by. A Beaux Arts fountain, well-trimmed plane trees and a small children's playground with a sandbox and swings are discreetly encompassed by The City.

I don't like swings — they make me dizzy. I remember a book of poems from my childhood by Robert Louis Stevenson with soft Victorian drawings of perfect children. The girls were swinging high into the sky and the boys rolling their hoops with watchful nannys nearby. I envied the subtle perfection of the children.

Les and I had been across from the park in Grace Cathedral. We had just walked the labyrinth with its perfect lunations and proscribed path into and out of oneself. The labyrinth always seemed to hold its breath so that no thought or action could be abused. Even when the great organ forced the walls of the nave, the labyrinth held its own, providing what we most yearn for — nourishment and our known place in The Universe.

The labrynth is a far cry from the swings that seem to have no purpose but to make me feel giddy. Up down, up down, up down, shifting the horizon to make life seem non-sensible, yet offering the temptation of touching the leaves overhead where the birds are safe and free.

Les is a big man, quarterback size, oddly graceful, an avid wrestler in his youth. We had met in 2000 over our common work in the fields of dying and death. He is a dear friend whose compassionate heart and sense of humor grace my life.

We came out of the cathedral into brilliant sunlight and the clanging of cable car bells. We were intending to descend into the cathedral's garage and leave. However, that seemed almost irreverent so we crossed the street to the park.

The air and light were fresh. Les insisted warmly that I let him push me on a swing. Visions of perfect Victorian children burst into my head, but I agreed. To my surprise, I found that being with the leaves and sky and flowing horizon made me feel safe and free.

THE PRISON

CMF

"CMF" stands for "California Medical Facility" in
Vacaville, California, where Bob and I helped
to co-found the first prison hospice in the world.
This piece was written July 31, 2006.

The main corridor is just under a quarter of a mile long, about thirty feet wide with wings like the teeth on a comb, right angling off of it about every 100 feet. The floors are a nondescript terrazzo and where there are windows they are fifteen feet up or wide and high at waist level — all are barred.

The Correctional Medical Facility (I always smile inwardly at the word correctional) at Vacaville is my sangha, my spiritual home. After twenty-four years, I am part of the "furniture" now. I'm a familiar face. Some guards at check points ignore me, one or two greet me with a smile and ask, "How was the drive (a fifty mile run) and did you speed?"

I know I am safe here. Safer, I tell friends who query me, than walking from my home six blocks down Telegraph Avenue to the University of California campus.

The prison is the state of California's main hospital and hospice for incarcerated men. It started out in 1955 as a worldwide model of care for prisoners who were seriously ill, either physically or mentally. It is now at two and a half times capacity — 3,100 inmates. It also houses inmates who are not ill. Many of the inmates are "three-strikers." The gymnasium, in spite of the overcrowding is still a free space for physical therapy equipment, Muslim prayer services, movies, and special programs.

Approximately 250 of the inmates are HIV-positive. Twenty-five years ago, at the beginning of the AIDS crisis, there were just twelve inmates who were treated like pariahs because they were carriers of the virus. Both inmates and staff were terrified of them, and they were isolated from the rest of the prison population in separate housing.

Dr. Elisabeth Kübler-Ross had gotten access to visit those twelve men in the AIDS unit. Like so many of her pioneering actions, she wanted to hear their stories. She came away from the meeting with a request from all twelve to have visitors. Because I was a member of her international teaching and workshop staff, I got a call asking if I would I go and visit one of those inmates. I hesitated (a step into a murky world that held violent snake pit Hollywood images for me) and said, "I don't know, let me check it out with Bob."

Bob, my husband, was a retired architect of 75, always a fighter for the underdog. Without hesitation he said, "Yes, if I can go too." A monumental life's journey for both of us was sealed at that moment.

We were each given an inmate's name, mine Kip, Bob's Joe. Each man responded quickly and eagerly, "Yes," to our written queries for a visit. We got visitor clearance from the prison. We set out from Berkeley for the fifty-mile trip on a hot August day in 1985.

Little did we know.

POLICE LINE DO NOT CROSS

Written in 2007.

There are approximately three hundred and fifty men I know who have crossed a Police Line. Some I met only a few times, thirty or so I've known for twenty years. They are inmates, cons, convicts, convicted by a judge and jury of a wide spectrum of crimes. Some really sad and stupid — possession of drugs, petty thievery to support their habits and some soul-shockingly violent. Many are Three Strikers with convictions that say your life is worthless, "Throw away the key."

A forged check is what sent Leo back to prison for probably the rest of his life. He is a small time crook, gay, suffering from AIDS and with the singing voice of an angel. I got to know him at Vacaville Penitentiary for men, he a patient in the AIDS Unit and I a community volunteer there. He played classical guitar, wrote his own lullabies, entrancing us all in my support group for his fellow cons who were sick. I haven't seen him in about a year. He's vanished into the long grey corridors, endlessly barred doors and windows with the sound of guards' heavy keys rattling on their belts or in their hands as they open and close doors and gates that never let you forget where you are.

Then there's Little Raffie, the opposite of Leo. He is an LWOP (life without possibility of parole) for a rampage of slaughter forty years ago in which ten people were killed. Raffie is one of forty inmate volunteers in the seventeen-bed prison hospice. Every week when I see him I inhale quickly and remember what rehabilitation and redemption are all about. He was in the Psych Unit for the criminally insane for years — endless therapy. He knows by heart all the questions and "correct" answers criminologists from around the world have come to ask him. He moves

33

comfortably down those long grey corridors saying there is no way he could live on the outside. The prison is his home and he devotes himself to recording books on tape for the blind and sitting with fellow inmates who are dying.

Bare bones here — it is a police state. Most live out their lives with no insight to their own hearts and healing. An amazing few, through their wish to serve, are hospice volunteers. With their compassion for their fellow inmates they find deep appreciation and love coming back to them, something they never got on the outside.

They acknowledge their crimes with deep shame and remorse. Their bones are picked clean, smooth and open to what each moment brings. They have seen it all and have come to a grace inside themselves.

This prison hospice is one of the most sacred places I know.

ANGRY AT GOD

Written in 2007 about an event that took place in 1980.

P aul was tall — 6'4" — courtly, and soft spoken. I had trouble hearing him in the noisy prison classroom, so I leaned closer into his intense face and dark eyes behind black-rimmed glasses.

"May I ask you a question?" he said.

"Yes, please, of course."

I assumed he'd probably be asking me about the ten-minute talk I had just given. That was the amount of time the prison had allotted me for that morning's presentation on dying and death and AIDS. It was 1988 and little was known about the newly-discovered virus. In the California penal system, as elsewhere, fear, rumors, conjectures and open homophobia were rampant. Housed separately from the main line, the 70 men in the AIDS Unit were victims and pariahs, the prison treatment of them a reflection of what was happening out in the streets.

Paul was one of those 70 men. He had come into my weekly voluntary support group just a month earlier, sitting in silence, but listening intently to the discussions.

Now in the classroom, as he began to speak, he leaned further towards me so that our faces were inches apart.

"Nancy, is it all right to be angry at God?"

I half smiled, thinking of the flip retort, "Of course, God can take it". But instead I asked, "What's behind your question, Paul?" There were several inmates nearby in loud conversation, so the two of us moved closer to a far corner of the room to hear each other better.

"At dinner last night, one of the men I was seated next to was very angry and kept swearing at God." Calling the 5:30 meal "dinner" was typical of Paul. He never took on the demeanor or lingo of an inmate. Paul, the quiet boy, who I knew was a classical musician and devout Catholic, was deeply earnest in his questioning. In response I said, "With all due respect, Paul, God can take it. I hope that man will seek out one of the chaplains here to talk about his rage and hurt. You could help too by praying for him. He wouldn't have to know."

There was a long pause. The classroom was half empty now, quiet enough so that his reply came across easily to me.

"Yes, I could pray for him. I suppose it could help. That's what happened to me the night I was arrested. One of the policemen came into my jail cell and prayed with me. My mother's blood was on my shirt and pants." His voice was soft and oddly flat.

My heart filled with fire! It took all I had to not step back from him. I knew he was testing me by telling me who he was. Would I recoil? Would I reject him? He had to know who I was. I put my hand on his arm and said, "Oh God, Paul, I am so sorry." With my gesture a bridge was built between us. He became a regular in my support group, still seldom speaking, but always intently listening.

Later, the chaplain told me that Paul had murdered his mother and did not succeed in killing his sister. His family had abandoned him with one exception, his uncle, his mother's brother. Once a month he made a 400 mile round trip to sit and visit and pray with Paul. Because of this, his uncle, too was abandoned by the family.

I have a photo of the two of them seated next to each other in the prison's Catholic Chapel. They both look directly into the camera. Paul's eyes without expression, his uncle's filled with compassionate sorrow. Paul died a year later of AIDS. He was twenty nine.

Hafid

Written in March, 2009.

What does twenty-four years of weekly visits to a state prison that holds 3,100 men mean? What do I know about the three hundred or so inmates that have been participants in my AIDS support groups? What do I know about the inmates who serve as hospice volunteers? I assist all of these men in exploring their own issues of their finiteness.

I know in a practical sense what brought them here. Most of them were abused physically, sexually, emotionally and by poverty as children. As adults, they have been convicted of a range of crimes, from the most heinous to simple drug possessions.

What I do not know is the cavernous loneliness, grief and rage that permeates every inmate. Everyone plays his armored role with skilled determination. I can see it, smell it, hear it and sometimes touch it, but there is no way to be it.

What I do not know reaches into every day as I go through the locked gates and then into the almost quarter-mile long main corridor. I head for the hospice that is named after my husband. In the opposite direction are three hospital floors, the books for the blind project, Special Housing Units (SHU), the criminally insane unit, and general housing. There is *endless* noise from the rattling of guards' keys and the opening and closing of iron gates and doors.

Hafid is wheelchair-bound now. He was in my AIDS support group twenty years ago. Up until two years ago, he was walking and a hospice volunteer.

Over the years he has always greeted me with, "Sista Nancy , how are things in Berkeley?" He went to Berkeley High and his "Mama" still lives there. She is too frail to make the hundred-mile round trip to visit him. Every week he tells me he is going to live long enough to get out and see her again.

A talented artist, Hafid painted the prison rabbi's office walls from floor to ceiling, picturing the hills of The Holy Land and an exquisite menorah over the rabbi's desk. He gave me a copy of the *Qur'an* one time. I thanked him profoundly but said "I can't guarantee I will read it." He said, "Sista Nancy, you will eventually read it."

After one of our weekly hospice meetings, he grabbed me and pulled my face down to his as he sat in his wheelchair. His face and voice were engorged with quiet rage.

"Sista Nancy they disrespect me at every turn. They strip-search me, they bend me over, they spread my cheeks, check my anus, check my balls, then they let me go through the gate into the visiting room to see my family. I am filled with shame, but I hide it. When I leave I'm strip-searched again. They bend me over, spread my cheeks, check my anus, check my balls. Not even my wife ever saw that part of me."

"They try to take my manhood away."

"Fuck 'em."

"Never"!

I can't know what prison means to Hafid. All I can do is be a witness to his rage. What can I know about what I don't know?

For Bob

STANDING IN A DOORWAY

Written in 2006.

The elevator had taken us down to the radiology department in the basement of the hospital. We had walked from our home just two blocks away, resolute, and questioning. Bob had been diagnosed with an inoperable cancerous tumor wrapped around his esophagus just as it bifurcated into his right lung. Radiation was the route decreed for his eighty three year old body, as strong as a human could tolerate, for six weeks. To what end? A cure, a remission, a reversal of fate?

As the elevator opened there was a pregnant eternal pause in my heart and mind — it was a millisecond where every part of me resisted stepping over that threshold — the liminal eternity that signified our life together had been changed in unredeemable certainty.

We stepped into the over-friendly receptionist's domain and waited. Shortly, "Mr. Alexander? This way please." A young man ushered him from my sight. I waited, waited with several others speculating on whom they loved and their loved ones' fates. My mind was dulled, panicked and racing. Bob returned with x-rays in hand and we were shown into the office of the head of the department. A slender woman, British born, kind and efficient, she reiterated the treatment plan for him. He asked, "What are my chances of beating this?" The doctor paused, his directness challenging her. She rose to the challenge, "Three percent". Bob shot back, "I'll take it".

He lived four months longer, resolute to the end, admitting that his fifty years of smoking had caught up with him, even though at my insistence, he had quit ten years earlier.

43

As I cradled his lifeless body the three percent chance was no longer relevant. We had both stepped over a threshold, he to his eternity and I to mine without him.

Fourteenth Anniversary

November 17, 2006.

We were amazed that we were in love. He, seventy-four, ripped from a second marriage of twenty-nine years by a wife who threatened to kill him from inside an LSD-crazed mind, hand scythe held aloft. He left, not by choice, but for a desire to live. I was forty-nine, resigned to singlehood after a fifteen-year marriage that died before it was born.

Our passion was filled with yearning, lust, joy, silliness and a deep awe that permeated the very sheets we loved on. Serious discussions began to ensue as those early months compounded our desire to be deep, deep and deeper.

"It's not fair, I'm twenty-five years older and will die before you. I don't want you to be hurt." (He had lost his first wife of twenty-one years, a train hitting her car.)

"So what do we do, fall out of love?" I queried. I reminded him of my childhood friend Nini. We had known each other from six on, three weeks apart in age. At forty-seven she was gone within three days from a brain aneurysm.

"No one has a guarantee on the next moment," I reminded him.

Like two dolphins playing in the wake of a great ship we swam into eleven years together. We married, I thrilled at being able to call him "husband".

Until the last year of his life he could walk faster, stay up longer and think more clearly than I. He sang, he played the piano, he designed cleanly elegant buildings in which people thrived, he wrote poetry, limericks and stories for his family and charmed every kid under ten whom he met. His creativity and passion for life were contagious.

We met at Big Sur. The edge of the continent, the ocean a mirror of self, one hundred feet up on a cliff you can see the curvature of the earth, a floating hawk, the mountains sighing into the sea, a rainbow made by moonlight.

He's there — ashes put into an ocean-bound stream — rushing — laughing — embracing him. Soon enough I'll be there too, rushing to join him.

My Rib

When I realized how much I loved him, for that moment on the sunlit bed, I was terrified. The slanting warm light from the afternoon summer sun crossed over my belly and fell to the floor and reached over to the couch.

He was away for several days, off to Los Angeles to tie up old memories and his absence gave me a chance to take a long deep breath and to listen to my heart. The last thing either of us had expected was this passion, this finding of selves, this safety and oh my god, such happy lust.

My studio was tiny, but we fit in it like conjoined lost hearts.

He was so handsome, a body like Michaelangelo's David with clear laughing blue eyes and a desire for me that was luscious.

I, having lived so long in abandonment, was reveling in this bonding. With the glory of his body in mine I had truly come to feel as though I came from his rib. My sighs and tears of ecstasy wiped away years of lostness.

But just for this moment, as the sun warmed me and the memory of him in me, I panicked. My vulnerability to him was complete. I had no recourse to rationality, no safety net, only free-fall in this small sunlit room.

He's gone 15 years now, but daily I remember our free-fall. As I write this, he's here — he's *my* rib now.

ROBERT

A morning poem,
a line to cast
a spell.

Letters in a row,
making sense,
to evoke memory,
of scent
of sight
of sound.
You were here
for a moment,

Held my heart
filled my body

Then gone
Leaving cast-spells
like eternal circles

Across
the pond of my mind.

A Letter To Grief

Dear Grief,

I see you standing in front of me, tall, slender, with kind eyes and long full rich white hair. You are robed in silver-grey cloth that falls softly to the floor. You reach out your hand to me and softly say, "Come, come, I am here to help you. Do not be afraid, for it is my job to help you through the searing pain of loss." I didn't believe you, but there was no other path to take. Everywhere I looked there was an abyss. Your outstretched hand was all that I had.

"Hold tight," you said, and we were gone. "Hold tight," you said again, "for you will eventually, each in its own time, curse your God, curse me, curse yourself and whom or what you have lost. I will collect every curse, every tear, every moan, every cry. I will not abandon you. I will bring you to the humanity of yourself. For in grieving - if you truly let me in - you will find your broken heart and begin to help it heal."

Oh, I didn't believe you. I thought I would die. I wanted to die, there was so much pain! In that free-fall you never let go of my hand. "I am here," you whispered, "I will always be here, but I will change and evolve."

That is true, you are here, but now you are like a soft cloak encompassing me, gently reminding me of how much I loved and was loved in return.

Always, your hand in mine, bringing me love.

Thank you,

Nancy Jaicks Alexander

꿈꿈꿈

GRIEF'S REPLY:

October 1999

Dearest Nancy,

You've learned your lessons well. Please keep on opening up your heart. I need you to help those in pain to find my hand — to grasp it — to not be afraid — to not let go.

Thank you,

Grief

FICTION

The Old Man

"What would happen," he said, "if you moved the 'L'?"

She was mystified. "What do you mean?"

"Move the 'L' so it's a sliver of a moon or a silver moon".

They were on the back stoop breathing the cool moist air — a soft evening — waiting for the doctor to show up. It would be a while because his drive from the other side of the river — providing the bridge wasn't up — would take a good half hour. If the bridge was up — who knows how much time — a sailboat or an oil barge — there had been talk for years about a permanent larger span but the town always voted it down and the elected officials knew where the votes were — so, no new bridge.

She looked at his face. It was in silhouette — his sharp nose and hard chin, just like the old man's. She had often wondered what the old man had looked like young — strong, determined and not kind.

They saw headlights and she grabbed his hand, but the car turned at the far corner and its red tail lights disappeared into the encroaching woods.

She let go of his hand — he had not held hers — just let her grab his — she needed the reassurance.

"He went peaceful — don't worry, we're safe — no one will know".

He had carefully studied insulin at the county seat library, not where he was known — he knew that just a cc too much would stop the life that had ravaged his for years.

He never could please him, finally stopped trying — joined the army and came back having seen how cheap and quick life can be. Killing — no problem. He came back knowing he wanted the old man dead. He wanted the house and land.

She had loved him since catching crawdads together as kids. She, of course, wouldn't have used those words — her sister teased her about her crush on him and then, "Oh you gotta boy friend" and then "Oh now you gotta wait for him".

And she did — dreaming of the sunlight on the hair on his arms — and then finally his return — a Purple Heart on his jacket. His wound had healed — she ran her fingers over the mean scar and wondered at his saying, "Killing is easy, you'll see."

One night in the cool grass, his body shinning bright next to hers and the full awakening of her first total trust of him, he talked about consummations.

"So many kinds of consummations. I want this place now - not to wait for that bastard to go. We'll do it — no one will know".

They fed him, bathed him, listened to his endless bitter talk — took one vial and filled the syringe —

"Dropped the other, doc. We cleaned it up and when he fell asleep we went down and ate. When we checked on him later he wasn't breathing. That's when we called you."

The doctor looked at the clock — 11:35pm — and made notes for the coroner — "heart failure".

As they watched him sign the certificate she caught his eye across the room, he knowing the land was his and she knowing that later they would make love.

FLYING

This piece was inspired by looking at a photograph of a
woman turning a cartwheel on a country road.
It was written in May, 2008.

There you are out of your body again! I sure as hell wish you'd stay in long enough so that we could have a sensible discussion. I know, I know you love traveling all over, but there comes a time young woman when you gotta come down to earth and pay attention to the realities here.

No, that was not Sallie. You know Sallie got run over right here last year. You just saw some dust dancing from the wind. Sallie's gone, she's not here, get over it girl.

You should comb your hair too. I told you that a braid would let your features show. What, you like the wind when it blows your hair when you turn over? All it does, as far as I'm concerned, is create more tangles for me to have to brush out.

Just come back down!

You were just at Shandy's? She's not there, she went to town today. Yes, yes, you went to town too.

Well, you know I believe you. You're out there flying around, but damn it I've got work to do and you're no help always telling me to breathe lighter and I could fly too. That's too scary.

I'll stay here and fix supper and you can tell me then how it was in Istanbul today.

MUSINGS

My Muse

"Ouch," said my muse as she bumped up against my resistance. "Look at all these bruises, years of bruises! It could discourage a less determined soul. I'm faithful damnit, I stick to my commitments, where you..." — her voice trailed off in my ear.

I had read the assignment for my writing class. God, Eudora Welty, you are more prolix than I can stomach. Not the story, but your writing about the story! Now, Ann Patchett's piece — that's more to my liking. Brief, funny and to the point.

But as usual, I digress. "Polish a segment... that originated in group on Friday." Well, I reread the tarnished words I had written on Friday and I didn't like any of them. None, in my estimation, were worth polishing.

My muse sighed, stepped back from looking over my shoulder, and went and sat down on the ottoman. If she were a drinking and smoking woman she would have lighted up and asked for a large shot of ouzo.

The usual battle lines have again been drawn!

EVE

Did Eve did get a bum rap? She was tempted by that damn snake and if I remember correctly, Dr. Freud — you'll pardon the digression — in your terms, a snake is a phallic symbol. So it was Snake that dropped down from the tree and said to Eve, "Look what I've got for you, you sweet innocent thing."

Boy was she a patsy. She knew nothing of the world this odd ball guy named God had created, or so He claimed. Created all of this in seven days? I've got news for you — it's been here a lot longer than that, but we won't quibble about a couple of billion millennia.

Then there was Adam standing around looking pretty vapid. Interesting Snake didn't say to him, "Hey brother, how about a little reality check. Do you want to hang out in this place forever?"

What did God call it? Oh yeah, Eden. Isn't that the name of an expressway, Eden's Expressway, that takes you due west out of Chicago? But whoa, back up, I'm way ahead of the story here.

Snake said to Adam, "How about a few thrills, a few rolls in the hay, a few nights on the town, you know a little fun before you're back to dust."

OK, Snake, enough. You know that it wasn't an apple, it was a persimmon. That vibrant orange jewel hanging there. You knew it was Eve's favorite color. You also knew as soon as she touched it, that she'd pull it off the tree. Its voluptuous texture would make her feel sexy and when she bit into it, well it was like mousse pie and it hadn't even been created yet. She did however know what soft bodies meant. She looked at

Adam and knew that if she didn't wake him up this *Homo sapiens* trip would never get out of town on that Expressway called Eden.

Now look where we are! Racing down that freeway to what?

Eve, Snake, Adam, God, Homo sapiens — we're all in this together.

Did she get a bum rap?

Your call!

MAGRITTE

This was written in 2006, inspired by
looking at a painting by Magritte.

A three-quarter glassful of water on top of a black umbrella floating in space.

"Why in the hell would you need an umbrella if you only have three-quarter of a glassful of water?"

A black umbrella — "Think Yiddish, but act British," a perfect description of my first husband, by a fellow Jew. Ed always, and I stress that, Ed always lived under a black umbrella. I left him. Fifty years later, when he died, I realized how much I still carried him in my heart. He got the privilege of my virginity, became the father of my two children and always, 'til his last breath, loved me.

Charlie Scribner, Jr. comes to mind. We met at a friend's wedding in 1956. The first time I ever saw him he was walking near the beach at Santa Barbara dressed in his dark New York City suit and bowler hat, carrying an umbrella. I laughed out loud at the sight of him. I came to enjoy and cherish his dry wit and self-deprecation.

If you are under the umbrella you can't reach the water! I see a child, arms blown off, now healed to pock-marked stumps that will never know the gift of touching a loved one's genitals, will never know the gift of lifting a water glass to parched lips — but that child will learn from watching the chimps to frolic with feet touching ears and lips and nipples and genitals and with the chimps, with tongue, will lap up the water as it is spilled and roll the upside down umbrella round and round and round 'til happy screeches and laughter echo in a turquoise sky.

"OUR BROTHER"

Written Christmas, 2006.

I spotted him as soon as I go out of the car. He was lying on the sidewalk almost in a fetal position, his back against the long sunny south wall of Walgreens where I was headed. It was a chilly, windy and bright day. He was protected from the wind by a false arcade and planter boxes on the plaza. People made arcs around him. He was oblivious to their quick looks and then their quick looks away. I paused by him. His eyes were closed, his feet were bare, covered with bloody and calloused patches. He had put his worn work boots together, resting his head on them as a buffer from the pavement. He was filthy with only torn jeans and a thin jacket.

I walked beyond him toward Walgreens and then I stopped. I must go back! To do what? I didn't know! Give him a twenty? I usually give a one or a five. But this man lying here, here in this bustling commercial plaza, exhausted, perhaps ill or drunk, but desperate enough to lie on the pavement against a warm wall needed - what?

I walked back, a folded twenty in my hand and bent down to speak to him. "Sir". His eyelids fluttered, but did not open. "Sir", again only his eyelids moved. "Sir", the same. His hands were clasped under his chin, covering a small satchel, so I put the twenty under three of his fingers, hoping when he awoke he'd find it.

As I walked away I worried. Would the money be stolen? Was he semi-conscious? Should I have tried harder to wake him? Should I call an ambulance? Should I take him into Walgreens and buy him socks, buy him food at the deli next door, and wash his feet?

He is "our brother"!

After shopping I met a friend for tea nearby and forgot to look for him when I left. I was stunned at my forgetting!

This Earth is "our brother". We must wake up, there is not a moment to lose.

Don't wait! Don't forget!

Clouds

"Who had the first thoughts Buddha?"

"Not I. You're looking for resolution?"

"Oh, yes, please!"

"Thoughts are like clouds and you know there is nothing you can do about clouds. You can't enlarge them, shrink them or make them go away. You can only watch them move across the sky. Your Mind is sky, so powerful — like the wind — it can be of hurricane force or as soft as a velvety breeze. The clouds respond — even when they are an encompassing fog - like a seemingly endless holding pen. The wind will move them on. Don't go with them — they will take you away from who you are."

"But who am I if I don't go with them?"

"You are Incandescence. By wit and wisdom you are in this form to see, to sense, to understand and to embrace who you are beyond the clouds, beyond the wind. You are Incandescent Sky showing The Way to yourself and others. Those are flourishing words — to simplify them — here, come, sit with me, here, under the Bodhi Tree and let the clouds go by."

MEDICINE BUDDHA

When friends are sick I often send them a tsa tsa

— a small statue of the Healing Buddha —

along with a personal letter.

Most of them include this information.

I began doing this in 2003.

This small statue is called a tsa tsa and it is part of the iconography of the Tibetan Buddhist tradition. He is the Medicine Buddha and He is the holder of the "spiritual apothecary". His bright blue color mirrors a cloudless sky that is eternally clear and forever filled with compassion, wisdom and healing. The healing can be physical, but most importantly represents that part of each of us that is our profound inner humanity that no ailment or negative thought or action can blemish.

The healing of our hearts and minds is the ultimate goal of the Buddha's teachings.

Place Him easily within your sight so that you can see Him at any time and be reminded that your spirit is forever intact. Nothing needs to be added or taken away — truly acknowledging your preciousness.

With love — Nancy

DEATHBED (WORK IN PROGRESS — WIP)

February, 2008.

Pretend I'm close to the end of my life? Who's kidding whom here? At 74 I'm close — closer than 50 or 60 or 70. When? The ultimate question!

"Deathbed" whimsy ties in with WIP. I am a Work in Progress. I'm testing my internal fortitude these 10 weeks of writing class. I'm really not sure I want to be here probing into my heart, probing into my psyche — looking for stories, waiting for a muse.

Come March 30th I turn 75. Three quarters of a century, not even a nanosecond in the Begininglessness of Eternity, but a long time to me. So many stories, so many personas. How many smiles, how many tears, how many breaths, how many changed diapers, how many heart beats, how many orgasms, how many fevers, how many cavities, how many hair cuts, how many lovers, how many husbands, how many mosquito bites, how many plane rides — does it matter? I'm not sure. So many questions — now I say I have no answers, but lots of opinions.

I am, with every breath, a Work In Progress.

I intend to retire on March 30th — let go of feelings that I have to save, correct, adjust, free, judge or write! I intend to watch and inhale with compassion. Maybe look at Goodwill for a pair of well-worn jeans to wear — go to the pound and rescue a pooch with one blue and one brown eye — old and sweet who would like to ride with me on the front seat of my Toyota and explore roads that are gravel covered and muddy.

Maybe I'll get a new license plate. It'll say WIP 75.

UPDATE ON THE ABOVE LICENSE PLATE:

Late in November of 2009 an inmate asked me, "How long you been doin' this?" "This" was how long had I been volunteering at the prison.

"Twenty-five years next year," I said.

"That'll make you an OG."

"What's that?"

"Old Gangster," he said. "Anyone who has done twenty-five years time is an OG."

My new license plate will read — "NJA OG".

POEMS

IRELAND

St. Patrick's Day, 2007.

Oh, the green oh
Oh, the vales oh

Oh, the stones oh
Oh, the pubs oh

Oh, the singing oh
Oh, the laughter oh
Oh, the secrets oh

Oh, the sheep oh
Oh, the weaving oh

Oh, the children oh
Oh, their cheeks oh

Oh, the horses oh
Oh, the rough lads oh

Oh, the bells oh
Oh, the swans oh

Oh, the sea — Oh, the sea
How it holds her
Unfolding voluptuous-green
Welcoming us — Welcoming us Home!

THANKSGIVING 2006

I stand with the mother who has lost a son.
I stand with the man who has lost his freedom.
I stand with the beast that has lost its habitat.
I stand at the foot of Christ's Cross reaching up
to gently bring Him down.

There is no salvation in suffering.
There is only suffering in suffering.

I want to hold All in my arms and say,
It is truly so simple —
Compassion for each story.
Don't buy into being a victim — if you live there,
You will become a perpetrator creating more victims.
There is no salvation in revenge.

Take your hand and cover your heart.
Just keep it there until
the terror of lostness diminishes.
It is a chamber for holding compassion.
We need nothing more.
Leave your hand resting there.
All that you need will come to you
Within its own good timing.
Keep it there.
Teach others the same.

You (A Love Poem)

It seems right,
Even just right

That I should love you in the Fall.

The air at one with itself,
crisp and warm.

The flame of leaves
taking breath away, both green and dying.

Then down, down to bare limb,
exposing all — going deep, deep, deep to root,

Where life holds and waits
for what Spring shall bring.

JUST ENOUGH

I thought I could cast a net

that would bring in the words.

Not so.

They are long gone, safe in locked boxes of memory that are only for me.

To use them now would render me crucified.

Each touch, each sigh, each glance was enough.

Just enough.

ABOUT THE AUTHOR

Nancy Jaicks Alexander is a retired consultant on trauma, grief and hospice. She was born in 1933 in Lake Forest, Illinois. She wanted to be a professional actress and attended Northwestern University's Theatre School. Her path from there did not lead to the theatre. She moved to San Francisco in 1953, and to Berkeley in 1971. She served on the KQED Board of Directors from 1976 to 1980.

In 1981 she spent a year in residence at Esalen Institute studying Gestalt Therapy, Encounter Group Dynamics, Psychodrama, and Intuitive Work. In the Fall of 1982 Elisabeth Kübler-Ross asked Nancy to begin training to become a member of her international teaching and workshop staff. Nancy became one of Elisabeth's "Life, Death and Transition" workshop facilitators in 1985 and continued working on that staff through 1993, shortly before the workshops were discontinued in 1994.

In 1992 she and her late husband, Robert Evans Alexander, FAIA, helped to co-found the first prison hospice in the world, at Vacaville, California. She continued to visit the prison regularly to work directly with inmates who volunteer to support fellow inmates who are dying. She retired in 2010 after twenty-five years of community service at the prison.

Made in the USA
San Bernardino, CA
05 September 2014